GOOD HOUSEKEEPING

Organize Your Life

GOOD
HOUSEKEEPING

Organize Your Life

Foreword by Jane Francisco

HEARST
HOME

Foreword

Who doesn't love a totally organized home where you can take a deep breath, stretch out your arms and completely relax? For me, that tranquil moment usually occurs the day after I've had people over. My family spends the hectic hour or so before guests arrive clearing surfaces, finally putting away that puzzle we've been working on, straightening pillows, reducing piles of books and magazines and tucking away school bags, stray shoes and dog leashes. When everyone leaves, the tidiness lasts — at least for a little while.

One of the things I've learned over the years is that more storage options and better planning significantly up your chances of staying on top of clutter — *and* make it easier to maintain a calm, ordered world. Enter our zone-by-zone approach to keeping things tidy.

Our ultimate organizing handbook breaks down your decluttering to-dos into smaller, more manageable tasks. Whether you're looking to take on every room in your home or focus on just the trouble spots (hello, junk drawer!), this step-by-step action plan will streamline every room — from the bedroom to the kitchen and even your closets. And once your home is in tip-top shape, our experts' keep-tidy tactics will help you maintain order every day.

We know that oftentimes the hardest part is getting started. That's why throughout these pages you'll find the most practical and proven organizing hacks from our labs and top experts that make decluttering easy. And the best part? As you decide what to keep and what to let go you'll also reveal what matters most to you — and rediscover the home you love.

— Jane Francisco, Editor-in-Chief

CHAPTER ONE

Getting Started

What Makes Organizing So Difficult?

It's all too easy for clutter to pile up in your home. Mail, books, school supplies, important documents and everyday items never seem to be put back where they came from. And then there's other clutter such as lightly used clothing that hasn't made it to a donation drop-off. Often, life just gets in the way.

By creating streamlined organizing systems to tidy up your home, you can regain control. Another perk: Studies show an organized home can do wonders for your mental health. So what's really getting in the way of your clean dreams?

"It can be various factors, such as procrastination, anxiety or a lack of motivation," says Angela Ficken, a psychotherapist in Boston. "People may also feel overwhelmed or defeated by the sheer magnitude of the task."

Meanwhile, Gail Saltz, M.D., a clinical associate professor of psychiatry at New York-Presbyterian Hospital, says throwing things away can feel emotionally overwhelming. "For some, it feels like losing that part of their lives or an old relationship, and it feels irreplaceable and therefore more valuable," she says. Both recommend breaking your home into smaller, more manageable tasks—that's why we developed a zone-by-zone approach to decluttering.

Each chapter in this book breaks down a popular clutter magnet whether its the medicine cabinet, or the junk drawer, so you can tidy up with confidence. Whether you need a complete reset with our 28-day challenge or quick Five-Minute Magic tips to keep your home in tip-top shape, these pro secrets will provide the solutions you need to have the home you love.

FIND YOUR ORGANIZATIONAL STYLE

No two people are the same, so why should their organization systems be? To find a flow that works for you, identify your tidying persona. For Cassandra Aarssen, a home organizer and the owner of Clutterbug, your persona can be determined by two questions: Do you prefer to store your everyday items hidden behind closed doors, or out where you can see them? Are you looking for a down-to-the-detail solution or a laid-back method? Once you've answered these, you can find a solution that works for you. "Working with your natural tendencies means that putting your things away and staying organized in the long term will feel effortless," Aarssen says.

How to Get Started

Set an Intention

For Kenika Williams, a professional organizer in Georgia and the owner of Tidied by K, mindset is everything. "You have to know how you want the space to function and how you want it to feel," she says. Before you start, jot down how you want your home to feel—think of these words as your organizing affirmation.

Write a List

Once you've set the intention, make a list of all the areas you want to tidy up. This will hold you accountable, and feel so good when you cross off each task.

Begin to Declutter

Before tossing or donating anything, audit your belongings, sorting through what you have. (Flip to page 16 for questions to ask yourself during this process.)

Start Small

Need a confidence booster as you begin? Start small and in places that don't automatically overwhelm you, like your nightstand or bar cart. "Get those mini-wins under your belt, develop a process that works for you and then move on to bigger, more daunting spaces," Williams says.

Time It

Fortunately, you don't need an entire day to organize your pantry or closet. "I tell my clients that 30 minutes is all you need, especially when you're trying to develop a process," Williams says. "Set aside half an hour, get through what you can and call it a day."

Treat Yourself

If you're dragging your heels on your organization process, give yourself an incentive. Once you've finished a zone, treat yourself to a small reward such as an episode of your favorite TV show or luxurious bubble bath.

Organizing Dos and Don'ts

DO Clean First
What's the point of organizing your kitchen drawers if they're filled with unwanted crumbs? Wipe down the area you're working on for the ultimate blank canvas.

DON'T Impulse Buy a Bunch of Organization Accessories
We love storage bins and drawer dividers, but it's important to edit your belongings and figure out your storage strategy before making purchases.

DO Measure Everything
"Make sure you get your measurements before you buy things so you're not wasting time and money to go back and replace items," Williams says.

DON'T Micro-Organize
Repeat after us: Keep the system simple. "Sometimes, the minutia and details of organizing can be something that people get in the weeds about," says Jeffrey Phillip, an interior designer and a professional organizer in New York. "However, if you think about organizing something on a macro-level, it can make the task more manageable."

DO Recruit Others
Unless you live by yourself, you're not the only one creating clutter. Get your partner, roommate or kids involved so everyone can stay organized together.

---

3 STORAGE SOLUTIONS PROFESSIONAL ORGANIZERS SWEAR BY

CLEAR TURNTABLE WITH TALL WALLS
"I've always been a big proponent of lazy Susans," Phillip says. "They're great for under your bathroom sink."

STORAGE BINS
Whether you opt for cute woven ones or clear containers, you can get a lot of mileage out of storage bins. "You're probably going to be using bins of different sizes and styles because [your needs] will vary," Phillip says.

LABELS
"These can help certain systems stay in place longer," Phillip says. "Whenever I return to a client's home, I always see that they're still abiding to their labels."

7 Questions You Should Ask Yourself When Decluttering

Is It Enhancing My Life Right Now?

Instead of asking yourself if you love the item — if it's in your home, you probably did at one point — think about whether it adds value to your life right now. Tag the item in question with a dot sticker labeled with the date. The next time you use the item, peel the sticker. If items still have stickers on them a few months later, it's time to donate them.

Do I Have Duplicates?

You probably don't need multiple white button-downs and 14 unused notebooks, so it's time to donate those extras.

Does It Make Me Feel Good?

You deserve to have a home filled with items that make you feel great. Boost good vibes by removing anything with negative connotations, like mementos from a past relationship or clothing that doesn't make you confident.

Would I Move This Into a New House?

Changing homes is a great time to cleanse your inventory, but asking this question now will save moving the items later.

Can I Consolidate?

If you're not willing to toss out a half-used box of notecards, try consolidating them with the rest of your stationery.

Does Someone Else Need This More Than I Do?

You might want to hold on to those baby clothes for as long as possible, but donating them might help a new parent.

Is It Expensive to Replace?

We don't recommend wasting money, but if you can replace an item for under $20 or in under 20 minutes, consider tossing it. (In the meantime, enjoy that empty space.)

WHAT DO YOU DO WITH SENTIMENTAL ITEMS?

From old birthday cards from Grandma to your son's first soccer jersey, parting with sentimental items is packed with emotion. "Consider taking photos or creating mementos to honor the memories associated with these items, or donate or sell them to someone who can appreciate and use them," Ficken says.

4 Ways to Get Rid of Your Clutter

Donate It

Many charitable organizations and churches accept donations of gently used clothing, furniture and household goods.

Recycle It

If you have items that are broken or no longer functional, recycling may be the best option. Many towns (and some retailers) have recycling centers that accept a wide range of materials, including electronics, appliances and even some types of furniture.

Sell It

Websites like Facebook Marketplace, Craigslist and Poshmark let you list items and connect with potential buyers. It might take some time for items to sell. But if you're not in a hurry to clear out your house, this is a great way to make some money while you organize your belongings. In the meantime, place your listed items in a vacuum-sealed bag near your seasonal clothing and decor.

Store It

Not ready to part with your wedding shoes or an old baby crib? Place them in deep storage, or consider a rentable storage unit as a convenient and secure location for items that you don't need regularly. Some facilities even offer climate control to protect items from damage due to extreme temperatures or humidity.

How to Create Zones for Your Home

Make a List

Sit in every room of the house and think about what you do in each space. Do you knit in the living room? Pack lunches in the kitchen? Note the frequent tasks of each room, and plan accordingly.

Think About Your Needs

Are you constantly shopping online? Are you a musician with lots of sheet music? Do you have an extensive collection of teapots? Those details make your living space special and personal and are zones that are likely waiting to be organized.

Run Through Your Day

Look at your planner and think about your routine. Your daily to-dos and schedule can help offer some insight into how you should organize or where to get started.

Go With the Flow

Organizing by zone is a fluid process, so you should move organically through your space. "You might start in a mudroom or an entry closet, but that area could also have an impact on the pantry," Phillip says.

Your Zone Checklist

Follow these handy checklists to get your home sorted.

Daily

Entryway
- Go through the daily mail; sort into drop zone, shred or recycle.

Living Room
- Fold and store living room throw blankets and return pillows to their places.
- Place remotes in an caddy or tray after use.

Kitchen and Food Storage
- Wipe down countertops and return cooking utensils or appliances to their designated places after cooking.
- Empty the sink every night (hand-wash dishes or fill and run the dishwasher).

Bathroom
- Straighten towels and washcloths.
- Check that shower supplies are organized in a caddy or put away.
- Store hair tools, skin-care products and makeup.

Bedroom and Closets
- Make beds every morning.
- Put away clothing and accessories.
- Have your child put toys away as part of a bedtime ritual.

Spare Space
- Avoid accidents: Store sharp tools like scissors in drawers.
- Place like items together. (Group together all sports gear, pet supplies, etc.)

Weekly

Entryway
- Rehang coats that have fallen and rearrange if needed.
- Place shoes and boots so they are easily accessible.

Kitchen and Food Storage
- Take inventory of your refrigerator before going to the grocery store.
- Write down what you have and note what needs to be used soon.
- Discard spoiled food.

Bedrooms and Closets
- Complete a visual sweep of these areas and remove anything out of place.
- Change bed linens.
- Tidy up the nightstand.
- Reorganize clothing in drawers if they've gotten mixed up.

Spare Space
- Unsubscribe to newsletters, clear out inbox and file important emails.
- Clear computer desktop from unnecessary screenshots and files.
- Take a few minutes to return everything to its rightful place so you can work with a clear mind.
- Empty recycle bins.

Occasionally

Entryway
- Restock your coat closet with seasonal layers.

Living Room
- Clear out your bookshelves and donate old reads to the library.

Kitchen and Food Storage
- Remove old food from freezer and pantry.
- Consolidate multiple containers of condiments and sauces into a single container for each.
- Wipe down your bar cart, fridge and freezer.
- Thoroughly clean cabinets and drawers.

Bedrooms and Closets
- Donate clothes that don't fit or are rarely worn.

Spare Space
- Go through files and archive or shred what you don't need.
- Examine emergency supplies to confirm that batteries are still good, equipment is functioning and food and beverages aren't damaged or expired.

Keep It Clean

Once you have everything in order, these speed-cleaning tricks from Carolyn Forté, executive director of Good Housekeeping Institute's Home Care and Cleaning Lab, will keep zones tidy and make your home sparkle.

Focus on the Floors
Dust and dirt can scratch and dull wood. Use a dry mop or vacuum made specifically for wood surfaces to clean quickly.

Deodorize Fabrics
Remove stale odors by sprinkling baking soda or a carpet-freshening powder on rugs, pet beds and upholstery. Allow to set 15 minutes, then vacuum. Start with a clean vacuum bag or dust cup for best pickup.

Dust the Fan
Tackle your ceiling fan with an extendable duster. Go over both sides of the blades, the motor and any lights. Or use your vacuum's extension and dusting brush to reach what you can.

Freshen the Bathroom
In just 15 minutes, you can give your bathroom a quick sanitizing. Use a germ-killing wipe or spray on hot spots like the faucet, flush handle and toilet seat. Keep surfaces wet for the time stated on the product label. While you let the cleaner do its work, straighten counters and put out clean towels.

Clean Out the Fridge
It just takes 30 minutes! Toss expired foods, then move items on a shelf to one side and wipe the clear space with a warm, sudsy cloth. Rinse, and repeat for the other half before tackling the remaining shelves and bins.

FIVE MINUTE MAGIC

Remove prints and smudges from windows and patio glass doors with a spray and a microfiber cloth. Alternatively, wet half the cloth to spot-clean and use the other half to dry.

CHAPTER TWO

Entryway

Before You Start

Think Through Your Flow

You're juggling a lot of things in your entryway: coat, shoes, keys and mail, to name just a few. Run through your routine: Do you remove your shoes upon entering your home? Place your shoe zone close to the door. Do you reach for the same coat repeatedly? Add a coat rack to make it easy to grab on your way out.

Control the Chaos

Your entryway is a pit stop, not a destination. "It shouldn't be a permanent home for things coming in, like packages or mail," says Carolyn Forté, executive director of Good Housekeeping Institute's Home Care and Cleaning Lab. "It should be a permanent home for only what you need to go outside, like your keys, jacket and shoes."

Shoe-Free Space

Keeping your kicks on in the house is a space saver, but shoes track in a lot of dirt (read: more cleaning). Avoid clutter at the door by designating storage space for family and guests.

Maintain Your Mats

Your entryway is your home's first line of defense from the outdoors, so Forté recommends placing a mat outside and inside your home. "Make sure you vacuum both sides of your mats," she says. "When you vacuum the back, it pushes out a lot of embedded dirt. Then you can vacuum that dirt up from the floor much easier."

HOW DO I MAKE A GREAT FIRST IMPRESSION?

Create a warm welcome by painting your entryway a cheery color or using graphic wallpaper. Monique Valeris, Good Housekeeping's senior home editor, suggests, "Spruce up the area with greenery, and hang art or a large mirror for quick checks before heading out the door."

FIVE-MINUTE MAGIC

Clean out your closet! This area should be filled with layers you wear daily, so shift out-of-season coats and less-worn items to your bedroom closet.

Coat Closet

Keep It Consistent

Swap out those thin wire hangers for a set of wooden or plastic ones. These durable alternatives can support and maintain the shape of your heavier apparel while creating visual cohesion.

Go Big With Bins

That top shelf is perfect for seasonal accessories, like gloves and umbrellas. Locate your baseball hats and winter scarves in a snap by putting them in labeled bins. Clear containers make it easier to see what's inside.

Back-of-Door Design

Don't forget about the back of your door. Use shoe organizers to stow scarves and gloves or hang hats on a row of hooks.

Pepper in Personal Quarters

Create stations for each family member or roommate, so everyone has a hook to hang their coat, a designated space to stow their shoes and a personal drop zone for daily essentials.

SPACE-SAVER TIP

No closet in your entryway? No problem: Store your jackets and bags on removable wall hooks. "They're great for backpacks and kid's coats, plus you can move them up as your family gets taller," says Marisa LaScala, Good Housekeeping's senior parenting editor.

Shoe Section

Add a Bench

Give your home a welcoming feel and a convenient place to sit while you take your shoes on and off. "I like having an upholstered bench for putting on shoes or resting a bag for a moment," Valeris says. "It's especially helpful for getting kids out the door in the morning."

Leave It On the Mat

Keep a rubber mat by the door so wet or muddy shoes have a designated area to dry off.

Close It Off

Want to keep your shoe collection out of sight and out of mind? Reimagine a slim dresser as a stealth storage situation. (You can even install DIY drawer dividers made with cardboard to partition your pairs.) If you have several people under one roof, consider assigning a drawer to each household member.

Consider Cubbies

Flip a wooden box on its side to create an instant cubby that you can slide under a bench or place in your coat closet. Each pair will have a home, so you'll never have to search for its mate.

FIVE-MINUTE MAGIC

No matter how careful you are, your shoes will track dirt into your home. "Keep a rechargeable vacuum close by so you can do a quick clean whenever you spot dirt, debris or pet hair," Forté says.

SHOE RACKS OR TREES?

Keep casual kicks that you use every day—your go-to sneakers and sandals—on a shoe tree. As for those fancier shoes, keep their shape with a shoehorn, and place them on a rack.

FIVE-MINUTE MAGIC

Already have a console table in your hallway?
Creating a zone can be as easy as adding a
catchall tray to the mix.

Drop Zone

You've Got Mail

If you have roommates or live with family, place each person's mail in a paper tray with their name on it. "You can also have an area for your kids to place permission slips, report cards and other papers that adults need to look at," LaScala says. To save space, Forté recommends placing outgoing mail in a decorative napkin holder.

Take Note

Ensure nothing is lost in translation and add a whiteboard to your hallway so you can jot down important reminders such as "turn off the thermostat." Or leave a note asking your partner to take care of dinner.

Hang Your (Key) Chain

If you spend more time than you'd like to admit tracking down your keys, add a small hook by your front door. You'll have somewhere to place them as soon as you step inside, and you'll never have to look for them again.

HOW CAN I ORGANIZE RETURNS?

Though the internet makes it possible to buy anything with a few clicks, returns are the errand that nobody wants to do — or can keep tabs on. To make sure your return gets in the mail, immediately print your shipping label, and place your item in its original packaging. Making many returns? Add a stylish wire basket to your drop zone, and attach a sticky note to each package to remind you where each one goes and their deadlines for return.

CHAPTER THREE

Living Room

Before You Start

Select Stylish Storage
Since your living room is the center of your home, shouldn't it look good? Store throw blankets and extra pillows in stylish woven baskets.

Performance Upholstery
Keep your furniture looking fresh by selecting performance fabrics, which are typically made with synthetic fibers like polyester. "They hold up better to washing and wear and tear than natural fibers," says Lexie Sachs, executive director of Good Housekeeping Institute's Textiles, Paper and Apparel Lab.

Move Those Must-Haves
If you're dressing up your coffee table, place those smaller items like coasters and chargers on a tray with handles so you can relocate them when guests come over.

A Pop of Personality
Your bookshelf doesn't have to be boring. Add a personal touch with framed photos and decorative bowls.

Pare Down Your Throw Pillows
Cushions can make your living room feel cozy, but you need only a few to add a pop of color and comfort.

Wow Your Walls
If you are short on floor space but have plenty of empty walls, level up your storage with floating shelves.

Conceal Your Storage
"Built-ins add visual appeal to a room while offering ample space for books, travel finds, games, family photos and more," says Monique Valeris, Good Housekeeping's senior home editor.

SPACE SAVER

Ease up on the furniture congestion in a smaller space by trading in the coffee table for an accent table. "It's a small detail that makes the room look pulled together and more functional," Valeris says.

Bookshelves

Find Your System
Whether you organize by color, author or genre, find a system that works for you—and stick with it. That way, you'll be able to locate your next read in no time.

Stack Them Up
Vertical versus horizontal books: Why not both? Depending on the space between your shelves, you might be able to store more with a mix of piles. (Plus, it will make a visually intriguing arrangement.)

Take a (Visual) Break
Fill two-thirds of your bookshelves, and leave the rest open—or add decorative items like a plant or framed photos. It will give you room replenish your to-be-read list.

Box Those Storybooks
If your bookshelf serves as the entire household's library, place children's books in decorative bins at the bottom of your bookshelf for easy access. For book storage ideas in kids' rooms, flip to page 118.

Curate Your Collection
Space is at a premium, but a jam-packed bookshelf might appear a little cluttered. Keep your favorite ones and donate the rest.

SPACE SAVER

If your stack of books to read is larger than your storage space, consider downloading digital copies of new books. You'll save paper and have a convenient place for all your books.

FIVE-MINUTE MAGIC

If you're going to add accessories to your bookshelf, place delicate items on the higher shelves so they're safe and out of arm's reach (or a happy tail).

Entertainment Center

Reconfigure Your Remotes

You'll never lose your remote controls if you keep them on a tray or a shallow basket. Place them on your coffee or side table to have them on hand for your next movie marathon.

Hang Out

Short on space? Make the most of your furniture. Place a cloth caddy on the side of your couch to store remotes, earbuds and spare cables.

Hide Your Screen

For some, having a big television in the middle of the living room creates visual clutter. Limit your screen time by covering it when it's not in use. Some DIYers have used a swivel bookshelf, but you can affix a set of barn doors or a decorative shade to the empty wall space next to your television.

Conceal Your Cables

A cord cover hides cables from your television or soundbar—and creates the illusion of a clean, blank wall.

Tie It Up

If you can't conceal your cords, try grouping them together with a twist tie. (You can kiss that cobweb of cables goodbye!)

Roll the Tape

Trying to distinguish between multiple cables? Label both ends of cables with colored tape so you'll know which cord belongs to which device.

Enlist a Sideboard

It goes by different names—credenza, sideboard, buffet—but this long and low cabinet is the perfect spot to stash your vinyl collection, extra art books and photo albums.

FIVE-MINUTE MAGIC

Yes, dust is clutter! Wipe down your screens once a week with a microfiber cloth to keep them tidy.

Coffee Table

Search for Hidden Storage
If you're in the market for a new coffee table, look for one with ample storage, whether that's a secret compartment or shelves underneath. "A vintage trunk can give your interior character and be used as a coffee table," Valeris says.

Top It Off
Since it's often easy to throw things anywhere, flip the script and make it harder to cause a pileup. Keep clutter to a minimum by displaying a beautiful bouquet of flowers or framed photo.

Go Big With Baskets
You don't need to buy a brand-new coffee table to get organized. If your current table has free space underneath, add slim bins to maximize storage. "If you live with kids, they are a necessity," Valeris says. "Put one or two in your living room to prevent toys from taking over the space."

CHAPTER FOUR

Kitchen and Food Storage

Before You Start

Assess Your Space

Take a good look at your kitchen layout and identify problem areas, like an overstuffed under-sink cabinet or an awkward, empty corner. Make note of underutilized spaces, cluttered countertops and inefficient storage systems. This will help you determine areas that need the most attention.

Establish Your Goals

Are you aiming to maximize storage space, improve your meal prep or simply declutter? Identifying your goals will help you understand where you need to focus your attention.

Sort Your Stuff

What goes together should be stowed together, which makes it easy to create specific zones. "I love coffee nooks that have your grinder, coffee maker and whole beans in one place," Nicole Papantoniou, director of Good Housekeeping Institute's Kitchen Appliances and Innovation Lab, says. "You have easy access to exactly what you need."

Know Your Flow

Arrange kitchen essentials by function. For example, keep cooking oils and spices near the stove, cutting boards and knives near your prep space and dish soap under your sink.

Consolidate Containers

Instead of having two bottles of the same ketchup taking up space in your fridge, grab a funnel and combine their contents.

Develop Healthy Habits

It can be as easy as strategically placing some of your groceries. "Leave a bowl of fresh fruit on the table and a pitcher of water eye level in the fridge," says Stefanie Sassos, M.S., R.D.N., C.S.O., C.D.N., NASM-CPT, deputy director of the Good Housekeeping Institute Nutrition Lab.

Countertops

Edit Down

More items on your countertops means less space to prep and cook. Keep clutter to a minimum, but allow for items like a saltcellar and hand soap.

Curate Your Storage

Keep similar items together in containers, such as a tray for oils and vinegar bottles. "I like to have a heat-resistant crock on my countertop with the tools I use all the time, like a spatula and tongs," Papantoniou says. "When your tools are positioned close to where you're cooking, it saves you time."

On the Hook

Attach a cable hook to the back of tabletop appliances, such as stand mixers and coffee machines, to avoid tangled cords while prepping.

Go Above and Beyond

If your cabinets are full, look up. Utilize wall space by hanging pots and pans or other go-to cooking utensils—Papantoniou swears by a magnetic strip for her knives—and keep your surfaces clear.

Make a Statement With Serving Pieces

Wooden cutting boards and silver platters are much too pretty to hide inside cabinets, so make them part of your decor. Free up some counter and cabinet space by hanging them from hooks or leaning them against the wall artfully.

Work Around Your Cabinets

Make every space work hard, even the exterior of your cabinets: Install a rack for wineglasses or mugs under your upper shelves, or hang a soup ladle from the side of your cabinet.

SPACE SAVER

Use a wheeled kitchen island for meal prep if you are short on counter space. Roll it to the edge of your room when idle to free up precious square footage.

Refrigerator

Shop Your Fridge
Did you know that nearly 40% of food in America goes to waste? To help minimize your waste, spend 10 minutes planning your next trip to the grocery store. "Take stock of what's in your pantry once per week, and think about what you can use or what's about to go bad," says Papantoniou.

Places, Please!
Everything has its place in your fridge. For example, cheese and meats belong in a deli drawer, while condiments can be placed along the fridge door. "Milk and dairy should be placed toward the back of your fridge [where it's colder], so they can last longer," Papantoniou says.

Don't Ditch Original Packaging
The internet might be packed with stylish refrigerator accessories like egg holders, but Papantoniou says to focus on function. For example, the plastic containers berries come in are designed to help the fruit last longer.

Crystal Clear
Place leftovers in clear containers so you can see exactly what's inside. "I have a cohesive set of food containers," Papantoniou says. "It makes them easier to store because most of them stack on top of each other."

FIVE-MINUTE MAGIC

"Every week, I go through my fridge and write a big X on something that's going bad," says Carolyn Forté, executive director of Good Housekeeping Institute's Home Care and Cleaning Lab. "I put them in one section of the refrigerator and the X signals to me that they have to be thrown out."

Eliminate Odors

An organized refrigerator doesn't just look nice; it likely smells good too. "I always store extra onions in a glass container with a strong lid," Papantoniou says. (An open container of baking soda can also eradicate unwanted stenches.)

Part Your Produce

Crisper drawers are a great place to store fruits and veggies, but it's important to place them strategically. "Different fruits and vegetables can emit different levels of ethylene, which can cause some produce to rot faster," Papantoniou says. "In general, keep your leafy vegetables and fruit separate."

Assign Your Areas

Label zones like "leftovers," "condiments" and "deli meats" with stickers so guests have a road map to follow when they help assemble a charcuterie board or put away leftovers. Plus, everyone in your home will be gently reminded where to put things back.

WHAT ABOUT THE FREEZER?

After you discard any expired or freezer-burned food, group similar items together. Freeze food in flat zip-top bags, label them by date and "file" them vertically to maximize space.

Refrigerator Expiration Guide

Terms like "use by" are mostly unregulated, and the sniff test isn't always reliable. Here are some general guidelines to follow when storing your groceries in the fridge.

Meat

Chicken 2 days
Deli meat and bacon 2 weeks
Ground meat 2 days
Pork 3 days
Shellfish, shrimp and fish fillets 2 days
Steak 3 days
Tofu: 1 week

Dairy

Butter Up to 3 months
Cream Up to 1 month
Eggs Up to 5 weeks
Hard cheese Up to 6 months unopened; 3-4 weeks opened
Margarine 6 months
Milk 1 week
Shredded cheese 1 month
Sliced cheese Up to 2 months
Soft cheese 1 week
Sour cream Up to 3 weeks
Yogurt Up to 2 weeks

Produce

Apples 3 weeks
Berries 3 days to 1 week
Broccoli and cauliflower 1 week
Herbs Up to 2 weeks
Kale and spinach 3 days
Lemons and limes 3 weeks
Lettuce 5 days
Melon 5 days
Mushrooms 1 week
Onions and garlic Up to 2 months
Potatoes 3 weeks
Tomatoes 3 days

FIVE-MINUTE MAGIC

Maximize convenience and reduce food waste by freezing your food in individual serving sizes, allowing you to defrost just what you need without thawing the whole batch.

Cabinets

What Goes Together, Zones Together
Group like-minded items together — pots, glassware, dinnerware — and allocate a cabinet for each category. (For example, pots and pans should go near the stove, while dinnerware belongs by your dishwasher or sink.)

Rise Up
Maximize your cabinets by adding shelf risers to the mix, which will give you an extra shelf of storage. (It's the perfect place to store glassware and canned goods!)

Go Deep
If making the most of deep cabinets feels difficult, add some makeshift drawers. Long plastic bins will maximize space and give you an excellent spot to stow table linens, cupcake holders and more.

Order Your Appliances
If you have a cabinet full of appliances, Papantoniou recommends placing your most-used gadgets at the front of your cabinet for easy access.

Let Your Basics Blend In
Store plastic wrap, parchment and aluminum foil in a well-hidden magazine file attached to the inside of a cupboard door. The result? Your food storage go-tos will be within reach but out of the way.

Follow the Straight and Narrow
Install a slim, pull-out cabinet in the skinny, wasted space between your fridge and the wall. If you'd like, add flair with a decorative handle.

Create a Command Center
Stick a chalkboard, a sheet of contact paper and adhesive pockets to the inside of important reminders, grocery lists, coupons, go-to recipes and the Wi-Fi password.

FIVE-MINUTE MAGIC

If your cabinets have adjustable shelves, raise or lower them to accommodate your appliances, keeping heavier ones on the lowest level.

Grab 'Em

Install a pullout shelf in a cabinet to keep pots, pans and pantry items within reach. Your days of pulling out everything to find one frying pan are over.

Double Down on Your Door

To avoid sifting through your cabinets to find a pot's top, add adhesive hooks to the back of your cabinet doors and hang them there.

Magnetize Your Metals

Save yourself a trip to the first aid kit by installing a magnetic rod inside your cabinets, so you can keep blender and food processor blades safe and secure.

Pack Up Plastic Bags

If a bloated pile of grocery store bags is taking over your cabinet space, stuff them into an empty tissue box for a handy, compact solution.

SPACE SAVER

Attach a magnetic strip to the back of a reusable plastic cup and stick it on your fridge so your kiddos can always grab a drink. (Just make sure your child drinks the entire beverage before sticking it back on the door. We recommend washing it daily with your dinnertime dishes too!)

Pantry

Handy Hamper

Hampers aren't just for laundry! Should you have some extra floor space in your pantry, use a hamper to hold reusable shopping bags or store food or supplies bought in bulk. Don't forget to add some labels too!

Group Your Goods

Place prepackaged nonperishables like chips and soups in clear bins so you can tell when you need to replenish your stash. Store similar items in the same basket, and add a label.

First In, First Out

After each grocery run, place your newest cans, boxes and containers behind those already on your shelves. That way, you'll reach for the oldest items first, so no food goes to waste.

Opt for Eye Level

Put healthier pantry foods like dried fruits and nuts at eye level so they'll be easy to reach for snack time. Meanwhile, store cookies and chips on a higher shelf. (Tip: Dedicate an area at kid height for bags of your children's favorite snacks so they can grab one once you give them the a-okay.)

Don't Forget Your Door

Add a wall rack to the back of your door so you'll have an extra spot to store canned vegetables and condiments.

FIVE-MINUTE MAGIC

Use a binder clip to keep unruly sauce and seasoning packets orderly and upright.

SPACE SAVER

You don't need a dedicated room to have a great pantry. Consider storing all your nonperishables in your largest cabinet.

Spice Rack

Temperature Check

Store your spices in a cool, dry place. "You want to make sure they don't go bad quickly and clump together," Papantoniou says. Additionally, she says, "Spices have oils in them, and they won't be the most flavorful if they're kept somewhere cold, like a fridge. Placing them right next to your stove can also risk them losing potency and flavor."

Alphabetize Your Ingredients

Store your spices from A to Z, making it easy to locate that container of paprika in a pinch.

Oldest First

Transferring spices into uniform glass containers "creates a stylish display"—and can even make it easier to store them—but you want to make sure you're using your oldest spices first. "Spices are one of those things that go bad, so you want to make sure you're keeping them as fresh as possible," Papantoniou says.

Customize Your Storage

There's no one way to wrangle your spices, but here are three options to consider.

MAGNETIC PULL

Avoid mistaking your oregano for thyme by mounting a spice rack to a free wall. This way, you can see all your go-to spices while you cook. Short on space? Try mounting a magnetic rack on the underside of an upper cabinet, or hang one on the back of your pantry door.

DEDICATE A DRAWER

If you have a lot of spices and some storage to spare, make a spice drawer. (Bonus: Since your spices will be stashed away, you won't have to worry about overcrowding your walls.)

LET IT SLIDE

Make that thin, long cabinet work in your favor by adding a sliding rack. Your spices will be easily accessible while you're cooking but hidden between meals.

Under-Sink Storage

Go for a Spin
A turntable container is especially helpful in corners and other hard-to-reach areas, like underneath your sink. Grab a clear rotating tray with nonslip grips, and load it with cleaning essentials like multipurpose spray and drain cleaner.

Let There Be Light
The area under your sink has excellent storage potential, but it's not well-lit. Illuminate your space with battery-operated, motion-sensor LED lights. These easy-to-attach fixtures can be installed in minutes.

Towel Trick
Mount a paper towel holder inside an under-sink cabinet door to free up counter space.

Clean Slate
"I add a mat to my under-sink storage," Forté says. "That way, anything that drips or spills doesn't damage the cabinetry."

Dry by Design
Give dishcloths, brushes, scrubbers and rubber gloves a place to dry by using a clothespin to attach them to outside a storage bin.

Drawers

Resist the Slip
Place a nonslip mat in drawers to keep utensils from shifting each time you open and close a drawer.

Store Your Stock
If your kitchen is blessed with deep drawers, use them to hold surplus take-out sauces and condiments.

Compartmentalize
Whether you're finding a home for your handheld juicer and can opener or all your dining utensils, you can't go wrong by decking out your drawers with dividers. "Shallow modular bins are great for smaller drawers," Papantoniou says. For those oddly shaped tools—a milk frother, a turkey baster—install a diagonal divider.

Optimize Your Oven
If you're not using your food warmer—or that drawer at the bottom of your oven—use it to store baking sheets and pie tins. (Tip: Residual heat is bound to come through the oven drawer, so avoid storing plastic food containers or any other items that may warp over time.)

Put a Peg on It
Dinnerware can go in a deep drawer if cabinet space is tight. The key: Install pegs to keep dishes and glasses from shaking and smashing together.

Curate a Collection
If you have some drawers to spare, dedicate one to your culinary collection. Store cookbooks or add dividers for your favorite tea packets.

The Kids' Corner
To encourage your children to become independent (including cleaning up after themselves), select a single drawer for them to store all their belongings like flatware and lunchbox-friendly storage containers. This will eliminates the need for them to ask you about item placement before they put clean dishes away.

Junk Drawer

Part Ways With Paper
Since most information is just a Web search away, free up some space by recycling takeout menus and other papers lurking in your junk drawer. If it's an essential document that doesn't pertain to the kitchen, store it in your home office.

Keep the Essentials
"Try to keep things that are related to the kitchen," Forté says. "Pens, paper and manuals for appliances are great examples."

Test It Out
Chances are, not every pen in your drawer works. Grab a piece of blank paper, test each one and discard any that aren't working.

Add Dividers
Junk drawers might be known for their clutter, but it doesn't have to be that way. Grab some small, clear bins, and assign a category to each: Pens and pencils go in one bin, paperclips in another and so on.

Decorate Your Drawer
Turn your junk drawer from chaotic to cute by adding a decorative drawer liner. The better it looks, the more likely you'll want to keep it tidy!

House a Home Hospital
Kitchen accidents are inevitable, so repurpose a small pencil case for bandages, rolls of gauze and burn ointment.

FIVE-MINUTE MAGIC

Loose change can quickly add up. Place coins in a decorative jar so your family has a designated place to add or take pennies, dimes and quarters as needed.

DOES ALCOHOL EXPIRE?

While unopened bottles of liquor have an indefinite expiration date, opened libations will typically go bad after one to two years.

Bar Cart

Lay Them Down
Store wine bottles on their sides. You'll be able to stack them on top of each other, and it will keep your corks from drying out.

Decorate With a Decanter
If you bought your booze in bulk, consider pouring your go-to libation in a stylish decanter. It's a quick, cool fix that looks better than a big bottle.

Streamline Your Storage
Turn your favorite piece of barware into a clever storage solution. For example, a cocktail shaker can hold stirrers, strainers and muddlers when not in use.

Create a Toast-Worthy Moment
Every home can benefit from an unexpected design moment. Dress up your bar cart by adding a vase with flowers or framed photos.

CHAPTER FIVE

Bathrooms and Laundry

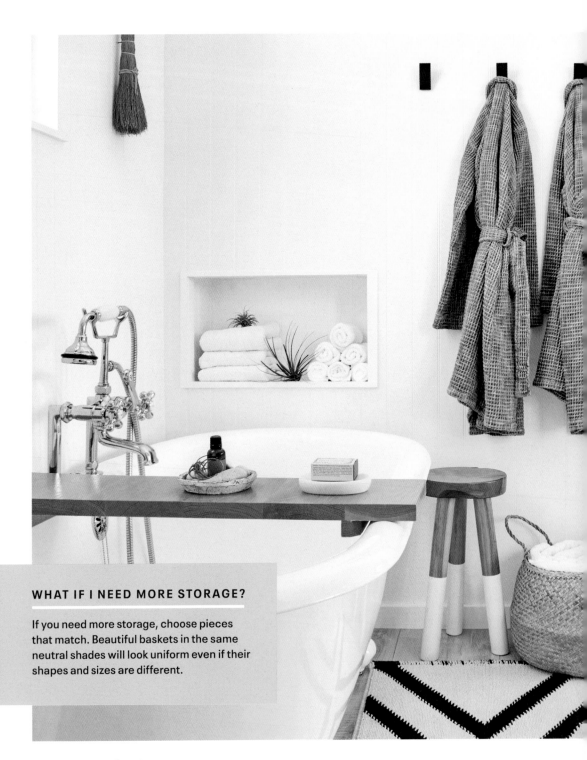

WHAT IF I NEED MORE STORAGE?

If you need more storage, choose pieces
that match. Beautiful baskets in the same
neutral shades will look uniform even if their
shapes and sizes are different.

Before You Start

Pick a Pared-Back Palette

For this smaller space, make sure you keep visual clutter to a minimum. Whether you're shopping for towels or painting your walls, softer colors will lay the foundation for a spa-like sanctuary.

Make the Most of Your Layout

Every square inch matters, so here's your opportunity to get creative. From hanging towels behind your door to storing feminine products in an over-the-toilet shelving system, the ceiling is the limit.

Follow your Senses

If you want to turn your bathroom into a serene, scented retreat, hang eucalyptus from your showerhead, add a dimmable light switch or for the ultimate spa vibe, plant a touch of greenery with a small potted orchid (it'll thrive in the humidity).

Keep Your Cosmetics Nearby

Place go-to items like your facial cleanser and moisturizer in a convenient, easy-to-reach spot. "I have a medicine cabinet where I store the products I use every day for easy access," says April Franzino, Good Housekeeping's beauty director. Products you use less frequently — like nail polish or a curling iron — can be tucked away in drawer or your hallway closet.

Vanity

Shatter-Proof Storage

If cotton swabs are a go-to item, place them in acrylic, shatter-proof canisters. These daily essentials will look good, and you won't have to worry about anything slipping from your wet hands and breaking on the floor.

Rock the Roll

Since washcloths are smaller than regular-size towels, they can be awkward to fold. Instead, roll and store them in one of your vanity's drawers — and place your body towels in your linen closet.

Reveal a Rod

Add a rod to the cabinet underneath your sink and hang a few cleaning sprays on it. This way, you can easily grab a tile spray when the moment strikes.

SPACE SAVER

Add a woven basket in an open under-the-sink spot to to collect laundry or to store fresh towels.

Keep Personal Care Private

"I'm not one for personal care products being left out; I like to have things put away," shares Carolyn Forté, executive director of Good Housekeeping Institute's Home Care and Cleaning Lab. "I have pull-out bins underneath our bathroom sink, just like we do in the kitchen."

Hot-Tool Hooks

Apply adhesive hooks or small bins to the back of your vanity cabinet doors to create a home for your hairdryer and curling irons. "A lot of tools now have Velcro attached to the cord so that you can wrap the cord around and then secure it," says Franzino. "If your tools don't have Velcro, you can also use a hair tie."

Keep a Go Bag

If you're a frequent traveler, stock three-ounce airtight containers of your favorite skin and hair products in your toiletry bag. (It'll save you a few minutes the next time you pack your suitcase.)

FIVE-MINUTE MAGIC

Clear everything off your counter except daily items like a toothbrush or hand soap. "We always recommend that people store their daily sunscreen near where they brush their teeth so that they remember to apply it," Franzino adds.

Shower and Tub

Reconfigure a Rolling Cart
Instead of using this movable storage for cocktail fixings or art supplies, roll it into your bathroom! It's the ideal compact size to hold extra towels, lotions and bath salts — not to mention it can be rolled away in a snap.

Double-Time Design
Add a second tension rod in your shower and use it to hang body wash, shampoo and conditioner.

Safely Store Sharp Objects
"I use a little bath canister to store my razor in the shower so it won't get grimy," Franzino shares.

Layer a Ladder
Lean a decorative ladder next to your bath or shower — and load it up with towels so they are easy to reach after a shower.

Shave Station
If your household includes someone who prefers to shave in the shower, install a floating shelf above your tub for your razor, shaving cream and mirror.

FIVE-MINUTE MAGIC

Use an adjustable shower caddy to keep your lotions and loofahs in one spot. It'll make bath time a lot easier.

Cosmetics

Clear Beauty
Store similar items such as eyeshadows and concealer together in clear bins. This way, you'll be able to see everything as you get ready for the day.

Look Out for Your Lipsticks
So long, lipstick swatches! "Store them in a small container and have the labels facing up so you'll be able to see the name of the shade," Franzino shares.

Be Careful With Your Brushes
Makeup brushes can spread bacteria when loosely stored in a cosmetics bag or drawer. Instead, keep them upright in a cute container or place them in a brush roll. (And don't forget to clean them with soap and water once a week!)

Elevate Essentials
If you have a lot of cosmetics—but only use a few items every day—store your go-to products on a small turntable for easy access. Look for a clear organizer with higher walls so nothing falls out. Items you use occasionally can be safely tucked away in your vanity's drawers.

Clear Out Cosmetics

"Once a year, I like to go through all of my cosmetics and throw away products I'm no longer using," Franzino shares. "Things can accumulate quickly!" When you do this, also consider tossing items that have expired. To find your expiration date, look for a small symbol of an open jar or container with a number followed by the letter "M." Most expirations are written in months. For example, a SPF bottle that reads 6M will generally expire in six months after opening. (Plus, Franzino says it's especially important to discard any expired SPF since sunscreen is FDA-regulated.)

FIVE-MINUTE MAGIC

Local charities often welcome hotel- and travel-size hand lotion, shampoo and other grooming essentials. If you've amassed a collection, place them in a tote bag to donate.

Cream Shadows 6 months
Fragrances 2 years
Hair Creams and Oils 1 year
Hair Spray 1 year
Lipstick 2 years
Lip Gloss 2 years
Lip Liner 2 years
Liquid Eyeliner 3 months
Liquid Foundation 6 months
Mascara 3 months
Nail Polish 1 to 2 years
Pencil Eyeliners 2 years
Powder Eyeshadow 2 years
Powder Face Makeup 2 years
Skincare Products Up to 6 months
Sunscreen 6 months

Medicine Cabinet

The Height Is Right

Get a little strategic about how you use your medicine cabinet shelves. Daily essentials like facial cleanser should remain at eye level whereas nail polishes and files can be kept on a higher shelf.

Pair With a Door Pocket

Use adhesive strips to affix a slim container to the back of your medicine cabinet door for sharp objects like tweezers, scissors and nail clippers.

Give a Boost

If your medicine cabinet has deeper shelves, it might be hard to see everything. To help, add some shelf risers so you can find that petroleum jelly tube when you need it.

Utilize the Bottom of Shelves

Looking for somewhere to put that headband you always use when you wash your face? Add a small hook to the bottom of a medicine cabinet shelf.

WHAT ABOUT MEDICATION?

While it's always a good idea to follow your medication's directions and expiration dates, studies suggest over-the-counter medications are still safe to take a few years later. (In fact, the FDA says that a medication's expiration date highlights when a manufacturer can confirm the full potency and safety of the drug in question.) Still, using expired medication can be risky, so consult your pharmacist with before taking.

FIVE-MINUTE MAGIC

Did you know that the bathroom's humidity can break down over-the-counter medicines and prescriptions? Place them in a hall closet or pantry where the temperature is more stable.

Laundry — Wash Zone

Don't Part With Original Packaging

While throwing your unused laundry packs in a clear plastic jar might look nice, Forté says it's best to leave all laundry supplies in their original packaging. "Boxes and containers list the ingredients and First-Aid information, which is important to keep on hand," she explains. "Also, original packaging makes it more difficult for kids and pets to accidentally get into."

New Heights

Place your detergent, dryer sheets and all laundry products on a higher shelf or in a locked cabinet to keep them out of sight and far away from kids and pets. Dress the shelf up by placing your cleaning solutions in labeled woven baskets.

Hamper Haven

Use large canvas hampers with handles to separate lights from darks in the bathroom — then move them to the laundry room when you're ready to start a load.

Skirting the Issue

Place extra laundry supplies under your sink. Cover up the clutter with a fabric skirt, then pull it back to find whatever you're looking for.

Style the Side

It's a good idea to keep your laundry essentials in one place for ease and efficiency. But if you're working with a smaller laundry room, affix a bin to the side of your stackable machines so all your sprays and scrubbers are within reach.

FIVE-MINUTE MAGIC

Place a container by your washing machine for change, receipts and lip balms that are lurking in your laundry's pockets. Make sure your pocket's contents are returned to their designated storage spot once the load is done.

Laundry—Dry Zone

DIY Drying Rack

A pull-down drying rack expands when you need it and disappears when you don't—hang it over a sink for drip-drying. If you prefer to keep your dresses and button-downs on hangers, add a tension rod so your clothes can air-dry. With either method, be sure to hang any drying rack from wall studs or a ceiling joist. The weight of the rack will be greatly increased with the addition of damp clothing.

Find Your Folding

Best practice is to fold your clothes as soon as they come out of the dryer, so create an area to do so. For tight spaces or top-loaders, consider a shelf that folds out from the wall, or place a butcher block on top of your washer and dryer.

Ironing Idea

If you have some spare wall space, add a slim sliding cabinet that can hold an iron and ironing board.

Styling Station

Put safety pins, lint brushes and a sewing kit in a small plastic container so you can touch up your garments as needed.

FIVE-MINUTE MAGIC

Don't forget to clean out your dryer's lint collector after each cycle—a lint-clogged dryer can easily catch on fire!

Care for Your Clothes

Follow these easy steps when sorting and folding on laundry day to keep clothes and linens looking fresh.

Now, Not Later

Whether you hang it, fold it to wear again or add it to the laundry bin, never let anything land on the floor.

Sort Smart

Keep colors bright and protect fabrics with three considerations. First, separate saturated colors to prevent darker dye from damaging lighter hues. Next, keep fabrics of similar weight together (that includes lint "givers," like fluffy towels, and lint "receivers," like dark synthetic blends). Lastly, consider the soil level. Extra-dirty clothing (think: sweaty gym shorts or muddy soccer uniforms) might need more TLC, like more detergent or extended wash cycles.

Shake It Out

Before you fold clothing, towels and sheets, give them a shake. This smooths the fabric and helps items lay flatter when stored.

Stop Pairing

Folding socks takes time when you're digging through a giant heap of clothes to find each one of the matching mates. Enter a gizmo known as sock clips: They keep socks paired together—from the washing machine to the drawer.

Fold for Wearing

Every item of clothing is different, but when you fold, "consider where you do and don't want creases," Forté advises. For example, don't fold sweaters or tops in half lengthwise. This will cause a crease to form right down the middle that will set in when you pile garments on top of each other.

Nest Your Bras

"If you fold them with one cup inside of the other, you risk messing up the shape and shifting the padding," Forté explains. Instead, nest them inside each other in a row, like you might see in a store.

Put It All Away

This final step can be just as daunting as washing, but getting your clothes and linens stored will make you feel incredibly productive—and keep clutter to a minimum.

Linen Closet

Fine-tune Your Folding
Roll and stack towels on a shelf for easy access.
Bonus: It gives your space a spa-like vibe.

Function Over Form
Place your odds and ends in clear containers with
lids so every toiletry, First-Aid bandage and spare
toothbrush stays clean and orderly. Plus, you can stack
containers on top of each other to maximize space.

In Plain Sight
Store everyday linens at eye level. "Beach towels or
bedding for your guest room really don't need to be
front and center," explains Lexie Sachs, executive
director of Good Housekeeping Institute's of the
Textiles, Paper and Apparel Lab. "The ones you're
swapping out more regularly should be easy to find
so that you're not ruffling through your closet to find
what you need."

Create a Divide
Prevent a towel or bedding avalanche by adding metal
dividers between each category. That way, your linens
will stay upright and in order.

Bundle Your Bedding
No more mismatched bedding! Place all items
from one set—flat and top sheets and extra
pillowcases—in a pillowcase.

Quick Question: How Do You Fold a Fitted Sheet?

Fret not: Follow these four simple steps to get the perfect fold.

1 Place your hands in the corners with the long side of the sheet going across your body and the top side of the fabric facing you.

2 Tuck one corner into the other. Repeat until all four corners are tucked into each other.

3 Lay it on a flat surface. (You'll know you're doing it right if your bedding's fabric has a subtle C-shape.)

4 Fold your fitted sheet into thirds—and voilà!

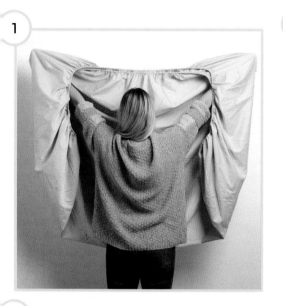

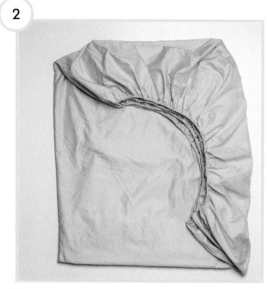

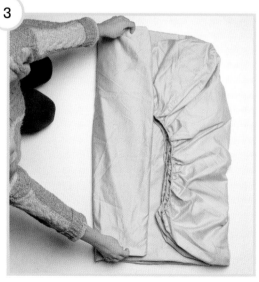

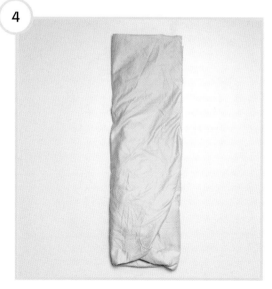

CHAPTER SIX

Bedrooms and Closets

Before You Start

Create a Serene Space

A bedroom can be your sleep sanctuary. Create a soothing atmosphere with muted tones and calming colors like a soft blue or a creamy pale yellow.

Elevate Your Lighting

While your bedroom might be filled with sun-drenched windows, closets notoriously lack a lot of natural light. Monique Valeris, Good Housekeeping's senior home editor, suggests illuminating the space with a stunning chandelier or a battery-operated sconce you can add with adhesive strips. "A well-lit space is inviting and set up to make it easy to see what you have on any given day," she says.

Offer Seating

At the foot of the bed, a bench or ottoman offers an inviting perch to slide into your slippers or simply sit for a moment. It can also act as extra storage space for linens and extra blankets.

Choose Hangers Wisely

"For a uniform appearance in your bedroom closet, try slim velvet hangers, which don't take up too much space and do a good job of keeping your clothes in place," says Valeris. "You'll be able to fit more in your closet, no matter the size, and shirts and camisoles will stay in place instead of slipping to the floor."

Nightstand

Get Extra Mileage Out of Your Bedside Table
"Nightstands can easily become cluttered with books, candles, jewelry and more, but if you have a style that's equipped with drawers or shelves, you can maintain order," says Valeris.

Buh-Bye, Blue Light
Keep your electronics out of your bedroom. Not only is it a good idea to eliminate blue light before bedtime, but it keeps your space looking clutter free.

Create a Catch-All
Every bedside tabletop needs a holder for rings, lip balm and anything else you may need nightly or first thing in the morning. (A small ceramic catchall tray or dish is sufficient!)

Hide Your Cables
Run a power strip across the back of the nightstand, so you can charge your gadgets overnight and plug in a lamp without cord chaos.

HOW CAN I STAY ORGANIZED WITH OTHERS?

Clutterbug's Cassandra Aarssen says compromise is key to creating an effective system with a spouse or roommate. "It's very difficult for visual organizers to remember where items are when they are hidden, so opt for open shelving, clear containers and large labels," she shares. "It's equally hard for a non-detailed person to maintain a very detailed system, so opt for broad categories like 'medicine' instead of 'pain reliever, allergy, antacids' and so on."

Under the Bed

Leave Your Mark
Label bins on their sides for easy viewing and identification.

Form Versus Function
While plastic bins work well if your storage is camouflaged by a bed skirt, consider a woven or cloth bin if they're hiding in plain sight.

Upcycle Your Storage
For a solution that's both cool and eco-conscious, incorporate old shoe boxes into your under-bed storage. You can also use old dresser drawers, but just make sure you create a lid with a slab of wood.

WHAT SHOULD BE STORED UNDER MY BED?

Free up closet space by placing out-of-season apparel in airtight containers or vacuum-sealed bags. Attics and basements can be home to mold-inducing moisture and pests so underneath the bed is a perfect place for out-of-season clothing.

FIVE-MINUTE MAGIC

Whether you leave your under-bed area bare or use it as a clever storage unit, vacuum that space twice a month to say goodbye to dust bunnies.

FIVE-MINUTE MAGIC

Minimize visual clutter by removing those claustrophobic, plastic garment bags from the dry cleaners. If more delicate items need protection, make an alternative garment bag by cutting a small hole in an old pillowcase and slipping it over the hanger.

Clothing Rack

Diversify Your Hangers

Use a different hanger color for each garment type to stay organized: For example, try black for pants, white for blouses and pink for dresses.

Opt for Inside-Out

"If you have an embellishment on a garment, you'll want to turn it inside out," says Leslie Sachs, executive director of Good Housekeeping Institute's Textiles, Paper and Apparel Lab. "It's less likely to snag on other items."

Store Your Sweaters

Yes, you can hang your sweaters! Start by folding each one in half vertically, matching up the sleeves. From there, place the hook of the hanger at the armpit. Fold the sleeves over one side and the body over the other. (Place bulkier sweaters on shelves for easy access.)

Double Up

Make the most of vertical space in your closet by doubling up your hangers. (It's as easy as linking two hangers together with a metal tab from a soda can.)

Tag, You're It

Instead of combing through your entire closet to find the blouse you want, streamline your morning routine by grouping like clothing together and placing divider tags between each clothing category. This idea is particularly great for parents who want to organize their kid's clothes. Simply grab a piece of cardstock and cut a circle with a slit halfway down the length so you can slip it onto your clothing rod. To make your tabs extra sturdy, "laminate" them with clear packing tape.

Shelves and Drawers

Snag-Free Solution
Roll trousers, socks and tights that are susceptible to snags in a resealable plastic bag. (You can organize them by size or color.) Slip them into an empty drawer for safe keeping.

File Your Fashion
Instead of stacking T-shirts and pajamas on top of each other, try the file fold, which will allow you to fit more in a drawer. To do this, fold your garment into thirds so it will stand up on its own. By placing your clothing side-by-side in a drawer—similar to a filing cabinet—you can find what you need at a glance.

Rock and Roll
Since silky pajamas and lingerie can get messy when folded in a drawer, consider tucking pajama tops into your bottoms and roll them together. Bonus: You'll never have to go searching for your matching set again!

Divide and Conquer
Stacks of anything have a tendency to fall over, so slip some dividers on your shelves. Typically made with plastic or metal wires, these vertical partitions will keep everything in place without the need for closed bins.

Streamline Your Swimwear
Fold your bikini bottoms into one of the top's cups to make it easy to locate a matching set.

SPACE SAVER

Create additional storage by adding hanging cubbies in the closet to store T-shirts, jeans or anything else that can be folded.

FIVE-MINUTE MAGIC

Group orphaned socks together with a large binder clip and place them in your drawer. Once their mate has been washed you can easily make a match!

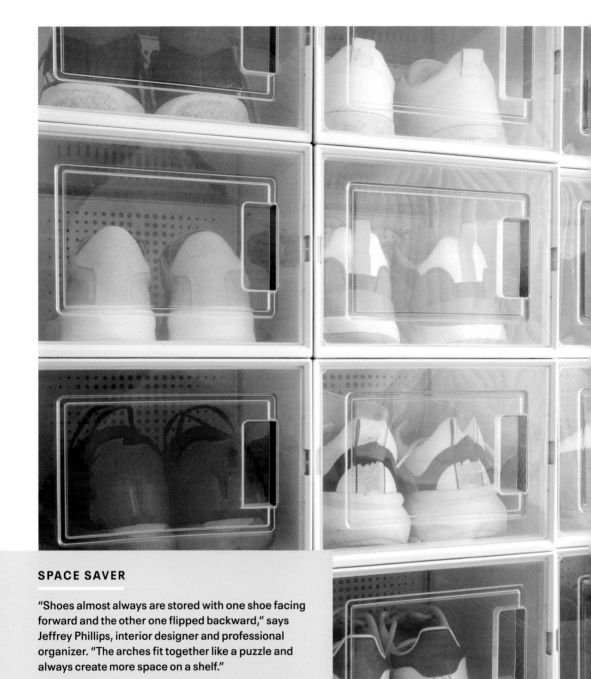

SPACE SAVER

"Shoes almost always are stored with one shoe facing forward and the other one flipped backward," says Jeffrey Phillips, interior designer and professional organizer. "The arches fit together like a puzzle and always create more space on a shelf."

Shoes

In the Clear

Place your sneakers or heels in clear plastic boxes, then stack those containers in your closet so you'll be able to see your favorites.

Photo-Op

While clear shoe cubbies are preferred, don't worry if you only have opaque bins. Create a label with style, color and brand of shoe and affix it to the front of your bin for an easy ID.

Bolster Those Boots

Tall boots can't help but flop over, causing some clutter on your closet floor. Stuff them with paper towel rolls or old pool noodles so they stay upright. Or, hang them with special boot hangers. Plus when they're stored upright, they'll keep their shape and stay crease-free.

Conceal Your Collection

For closets that are on the smaller side, consider alternative solutions to stow your shoes in the bedroom. Place flip-flops and flats in an upholstered ottoman with hidden storage. (It'll double as a convenient place to sit!) Alternatively, place flat sandals upright in a storage bin which will allow you to store more and easily spot the pair you want to wear.

Handbags, Jewelry and Accessories

Show Off Your Scarves
You'll be more likely to accessorize if you can see your options, so place a few of your beanies or gloves in a glass bowl or vase on a shelf.

Revive the Tension Rod
Use a tension rod to hang belts and ties. You'll free up shelf space and be able to see all your options.

Hip Hooks
Hooks help to organize hands and headbands, bags and necklaces. Plus, this clever storage trick will double as chic closet decor.

Ring a Ding
Create individual holders for your scarf collection by placing a few shower rings on an empty hanger. Drape one scarf through each ring to minimize knots and wrinkles.

Line It Up
Maximize your shelves by lining your favorite purses next to each other. You'll be able to fit more bags in your space—not to mention you'll be able to easily locate every tote and clutch.

Try Velvet Trays
Available in a variety of sizes and configurations, velvet trays offer a great way to sort your jewelry. Also, they'll help protect your pieces from scuffs and scratches.

Stash Away Smaller Items
If your built-in closet has extra storage space, dedicate a drawer to smaller items like sunglasses or barrettes. "You can rely on drawer organizers for smaller accessories to give your closet a custom, luxe feel and prevent clutter on any counters," Valeris says.

HOW DO YOU UNTANGLE JEWELRY?

Use a straight pin to gently pull out all the knots. If that doesn't work, try placing the necklace on a hard, nonporous surface such as glass. Once you apply a few drops of baby oil or mineral oil to the chain, try the pin again to work through those kinks.

Kids' Room

Keep It Simple
Keep the organization routines in your children's bedroom as easy as possible. "It's not the amount of organization, it's finding the level of organization that kids can actually handle on their own," says Marisa LaScala, Good Housekeeping's senior parenting editor. "If you try to implement a system that's too complicated or time-consuming, they just won't do it and you'll wind up cleaning up by yourself." For example, instead of asking your kid to separate their white and dark clothing, give them one laundry bin so dirty clothing is not on the ground.

Level Up With a Lofted Bed
Make the most of their small space with a lofted bed. This vertical will free up some in-demand floor space, so you can store everything from an art easel to out-of-season clothing.

Organize by Age
Sachs uses the higher shelves in her daughters' closets to store clothes that don't fit them yet. "Whenever the seasons change, I check that shelf to see which items are now the right size," she shares. "When my older one grows out of her clothes, I sort them by size in storage bins and save them for her younger sister."

Give Their Walls an Art Gallery Edge

If you're looking for a way to show off your kids' most recent artwork in their room, LaScala recommends hanging up a magnetic white board to avoid clutter. "It's like a fridge that's just for our daughter," she adds. "We refresh it once a season!"

Build Their Book Collection

Adding floating shelves or picture ledges to their walls — and fill them with your kids' favorite books! Your kids will have a blast choosing books to read and it'll double as a cool alternative for wall art!

Sort Accessories by Occasion

With so many hats, bows and costumes to sift through, organizing your kids' accessories can feel like an uphill battle. LaScala suggests sorting by how often your child wears them. "My daughter has a jewelry box filled with what she wears most. The things she saves for 'special occasions' are in another and dress-up jewelry is in another."

Tag, You're It

Streamline your morning routine by placing divider tags between each clothing category, like dresses and tops. This idea is particularly great for parents who want to organize their kids' clothes. (Simply grab a piece of cardboard paper and cut a circle with a slit halfway down the length so you can slip it onto your clothes rod. To make your tabs extra sturdy, "laminate" them with clear packing tape.)

HOW DO I GET MY KIDS INVOLVED IN ORGANIZING?

Give your kids a chance to look around the room and show you what's there. Maeve Richmond, a professional organizing coach, says this builds trust. "I get a sense of their language and tone, which can illuminate things that are important to them."

CHAPTER SEVEN

Spare Space

Before You Start

Be Careful About Contents

It's tempting to store all your miscellaneous belongings in your basement or attic; however, these spaces are neither climate- nor pest-controlled, so exercise caution. Keep flammable paints, delicate fabrics, important papers and food out of these zones.

Manage Your Moisture

Your basement's humid air can cause items to smell musty or even damage wooden furniture. Keep items intact by picking up a dehumidifier or humidifier and keep your levels around 40% to 50%.

Pest-Free Place

"Seal off any entry points to the garage by installing weather stripping under the garage door to keep pests out," says Dan DiClerio, director of Good Housekeeping Institute's Home Improvement and Outdoor Lab.

Work-Life Balance

Unless you're lucky enough to have a dedicated room, it's likely your "home office" is a corner of your bedroom or living room—and nobody wants to stare at their work essentials after they've clocked out. Place your laptop and important notes in a spare drawer. If you have the space, use a wheeled cart to store work items so you can roll it into your closet at the end of the day.

WHAT ARE SPARE SPACES?

We all have that *one* multipurpose room that, despite our best efforts, can feel overwhelming to keep tidy. Instead of treating these spare spaces as catch-all places, assign each room one or two zones. Suddenly, your basement isn't a miscellaneous room: It's your home gym and holiday decoration storage. While everyone's spare space will look different, we're rounding up a few classic zone ideas to get you started.

Home Gym

Bust Out a Basket
Store exercise mats and yoga blocks in a plastic bin — bonus points if your basket can stand up on its own!

Add a Strap
Speaking of your yoga mat, keep yours from rolling open by wrapping your exercise strap around it. You're reducing visual clutter and giving your exercise strap a home. It's a win-win.

Revamp Your Workout Rack
Repurpose a simple wire shoe rack to hold dumbbells, cycling shoes and water bottles.

Off the Hook
"Adhesive hooks are your friend," advises Zee Krstic, Good Houskeeping's former health editor. "Even if it's a specific hook for a specific item like a resistance band, it's really helpful."

Contain Yourself
Use clear jars with lids to keep hair ties and blister bandages close by.

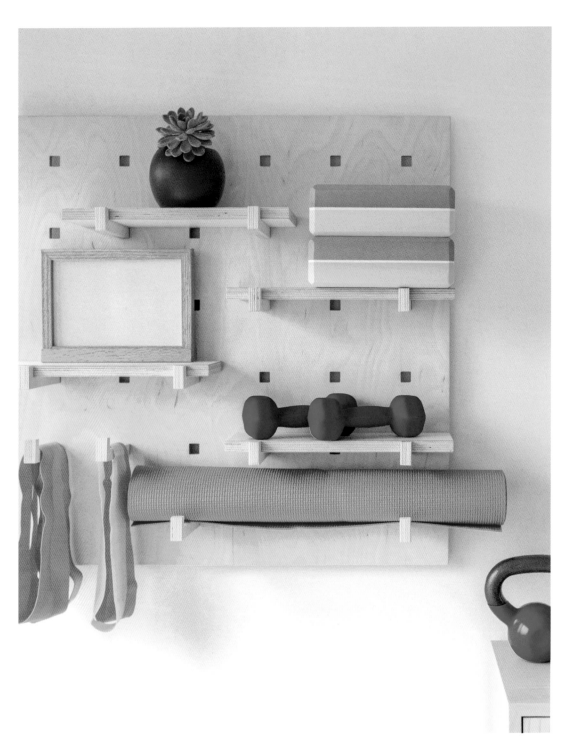

Wall-to-Wall Workout

"You'll be surprised at how you can seamlessly blend design and function together by adding storage to your wall space," Krstic shares. "In my hallway, I have converted a wall-mounted file folder into an organizer for fitness must-haves like sweatbands and hats."

Easy-to-Reach Water Break

Have multiple family members using your gym zone? Keep water bottles organized and easily accessible by placing them on a small wine rack. Whether they're practicing karate moves or perfecting their dance for that big talent show, they won't be far from a well-deserved water break. (Just make sure your gym is near a faucet!)

Clean-Up Crew

Extend your equipment's lifespan by keeping it clean. For easy access, place your sprays, wipes and cleaners in a portable caddy so you can wipe down your equipment after each use.

FIVE MINUTE MAGIC

Lay down interlocking mat tiles to protect your floor — and knees! "Your home gym should not incorporate carpeting," says Krstic. "Carpet absorbs sweat easier than you think and can hold onto stinky musky odors unlike other surfaces in your home."

Seasonal Decor Storage

Merry and Bright

Save yourself the time (and headache) of untangling holiday lights by tightly wrapping your strand around a piece of cardboard.

Show Off Your Season

Large plastic totes come color-coded so you can distinguish Easter and Halloween decorations from Hanukkah and Christmas ones. Not to mention they can fit nicely on basement or attic shelves.

Organized Ornaments

Tuck small ornaments in cleaned-out egg cartons. Instead of tossing out used tissue paper with the recycling, use it as extra packing material to cushion breakable bulbs in containers.

Seal Your Inflatables

Once you wipe down and dry your inflatable yard decor, fold and store them in a vacuumed-sealed bag to save space.

Treat Your Tree

Keep your artificial Christmas tree clean and protected all year long with a roll of shrink wrap. Once you're ready to decorate, simply cut the wrap and fluff up its branches.

FIVE-MINUTE MAGIC

Create a holiday backup kit with ornament hooks, tacks and replacement bulbs. (Psst...Most of them go on sale after the special season.)

Craft Station

Color Me Happy

Spark a little bit of joy in your crafts zone by arranging your supplies by color. (For example, place red construction paper next to orange construction paper and so on.) It's an aesthetically pleasing move that makes it easy to spot your desired buttons, poms-poms and glitter containers.

Jazz It Up With Jars

Clear jars make excellent storage solutions for small objects like pens, pencils and pipe cleaners. They also double as decor, adding instant color to any space.

Make It Mounted

Since you'll need as much table space as possible to complete that DIY project or science experiment with the kids, mount your supplies. Floating shelves, pegboard walls and smaller cubbies will take your craft tools to new heights — literally.

On a Roll

For a move that's pretty and practical, hang spools of ribbon from a tension rod.

Safekeep Your Scraps

Perfect for the scrapbooker: Store paper, cut-outs and stickers in three-ring binders. Use clear sheet protectors to keep all your scrapbooking materials in tip-top shape.

Toy Zone

Over the Rainbow
Color-coded art supplies give you and your kids an easy way to stay tidy, and the little ones can learn about Roy G. Biv in the process.

Create a Cage
"I love toy zoos because they hold a lot of stuffed animals," says Marisa LaScala, Good Housekeeping's senior parenting editor. "The kids can see where their favorite ones are and reach in through the bungee cords to grab them." To create your own, build a vertical, four-sided frame with wooden planks and add lines of shock cord from the base of the zoo to the top.

Mix It All Together
Keep packaging to a minimum by storing toys in clear plastic bins. No need to organize toys perfectly: Though it may seem odd to use one bin for blocks and plastic tomatoes from their play kitchen, mixing and matching toys can enhance kids' creativity.

FIVE-MINUTE MAGIC

"Set a timer and tell your kids to put their belongings away for a few minutes," says LaScala.

Packable Pouches

Cut down on bulky boxes by placing game boards and puzzle pieces in silicone zippered bags. Just don't forget to keep the game directions or take a picture of the puzzle's final product.

Runway-Ready

Give their costumes a fashionable moment by hanging their favorite dress-up ensembles on hooks. Have lots of costumes? A mini rolling rack is an adorable-yet-effective alternative.

Try a Tilt

You can only put so many bins on top of your cabinets. Instead, pick up a tilted bin unit so your little ones can see exactly what's inside and can grab toys on their own.

HOW DO I KEEP MY KIDS' SPACES ORGANIZED?

As LaScala says, routine is key. "It's important to have a morning routine as well as a system they use when they get home from school," she shares. "Think about where the backpack goes as well as where the homework and important papers go. It takes time to set up, but it eventually becomes part of being in the family."

Home Office

Take Charge
Paper can pile up fast. "If you read it and decide you don't need it, immediately put it in the shredder or recycling bin," recommends Carolyn Forté, executive director of Good Housekeeping Institute's Home Care and Cleaning Lab. If it's something that needs follow up, practice ART: Action, Reference, Trash. Use letter trays for action items, a filing cabinet for reference items and a shredder for trash.

Streamline Your Supplies
If your desk has few or no drawers, group necessary tools and accessories together on a tray that you can simply move aside when you need room to spread out. (Even better? You don't need to buy office supplies: Use an empty candle canister for pens and pencils or a spare tray for paper clips.)

Go Paperless
Convert bills and invoices into digital format. Not only are free tech tools like Dropbox and Evernote excellent places to stow your records, but they're both Good Housekeeping Institute-approved.

Display Your To-Do List

Out-of-sight, out-of-mind might be a great mindset for some areas of your life—but not your workspace. Place papers that need priority attention in a tray near your entryway or desk. They'll be harder to ignore when you pass them every day.

Protect Your Important Papers

Place your birth certificate, marriage license and other important physical papers in a fire-safe box for ultimate protection.

Create a Charging Center

Grab a multi-port USB hub to always keep your devices powered-up and nearby. Plus, you'll never have to go searching for your wireless headphones' charging cable again.

WHAT CAN I DO WITH PHOTOS?

Nowadays, most of us take pictures on our smartphones or digital cameras. However, if you have some physical prints lying around, store them in photo boxes. Label each box by year—and include negatives and photo discs inside, too.

Computer

Step Up Your Security
"Strengthen passwords with at least 12+ characters and random words and numbers, not birthdays and pet names," recommends Rachel Rothman, Good Houskeeping's chief technologist and executive technical director.

Protect Your Passwords
To keep your passwords safe, secure and accessible, Rothman recommends a platform called 1Password. "It helps you build and remember strong passwords, and you only have to remember the main one to unlock access," she explains.

Blank Slate
"While desktop backgrounds can feel personal and inspiring, try to choose one that won't add more visual distraction and clutter and confusion to your screen," Rothman says. "You can even choose a background that will play into your folder structure—like four boxes of color."

Back it Up
According to computer storage brand Apricorn, over 50 percent of people can't remember the last time they backed up their computer. Even worse, another company called Acronis found that over 65 percent of people accidentally lost data from their computer. Beat the odds—and clear up your desktop—by picking up an external hard drive or uploading everything onto an online server.

File Away

It doesn't matter if you're digitizing old photos or cleaning out your inbox, never underestimate the power of digital folder. Since space is virtually infinite on the cloud, feel free to get as specific as you'd like with your files. (Corral all your emails from one specific work project in a folder or dedicate a specific space for photos that are particularly special.)

Think Beyond Inbox Zero

While inbox zero is possible, Rothman recommends developing a system that can improve your productivity. "I spend focused time responding to important emails when I can give undivided attention, and other time handling 'two-minute emails," she shares. "I batch this way to maintain necessary focus and minimize distractions."

Automate Your Life

Sometimes, the best organization solutions are the ones you don't have to think about. Sign up for platforms that do the digital legwork for you. For example, Calendly shows your availability to colleagues and clients — and adds new appointments directly to your calendar. Meanwhile, Google has a filter feature where you can automatically have certain emails labeled, forwarded or marked as read.

HOW DO I ORGANIZE MY SMARTPHONE?

Research from tech company Asurion suggests that the average American checks their phone 96 times a day — so it's important that your screen is organized, too. "The first page of apps is dedicated to my most used; it saves me time on those high use apps," Rothman says. "My dock is customized for my most used four: Text, phone, camera and my web browser." She also recommends consolidating similar apps like social media or travel programs into folders for easy access.

Tool Shed

Style With Slat Walls

"I'm a big fan of slat wall systems, which are relatively affordable, easy to install, and they allow you to store your tools in plain sight with the help of hooks, baskets and other accessories," DiClerico says. "It's a step up from pegboard, which offers similar vertical storage but with fewer accessory options."

Keep Your Cases

Since most power tools come with other blades and bits, store them in the carrying cases they come with. Exercise caution by placing the tools up high on shelves to keep them far away from little hands.

Hot Wheels

"Tool cabinets on wheels are another option," DiClerico adds. "It's worth it if you have a lot of expensive tools, since you won't have to worry about them falling to the ground and getting damaged."

Make It Work With Magnets

Add a magnetic strip to keep those nuts and bolts on-hand and off your floor.

Bundle Your Boxes

If you want to save boxes for your electronics and small appliances, those broken-down boxes, create clutter. Forté recommends reducing the visual chaos by tying your cardboard scraps together with a bungee cord.

HOW DO I STORE HAZARDOUS MATERIALS?

Spare spaces are a great place for paint cans and toxic cleaners, but you need to store them safely. "Paint shouldn't go in a garage because temperature swings can degrade it," DiClerico explains. "Gasoline and fuel-powered tools should best kept in an outdoor shed: Garages often have equipment with pilot lights, like a water heater. Vapors from stored fuel could react with the open flame and cause an explosion."

Garden and Patio Essentials

Cover Up
In a dream world, you'd be able to move all outdoor furniture inside once the temperature drops. But if that's not possible, protect them from the elements by fastening a bungee cord around a thick, water-resistant tarp.

Access the Edibility
Place green stickers on plant markers when a plant is edible and red for what isn't.

Wind it Up
Think of a garden hose as the outdoor equivalent to a gadget's cable. To keep your space neat and organized, place your hose on a wall-mounted reel or wheeled caddy.

Protect Your Patio Essentials
If your garage is on the smaller side, keep outdoor toys and patio furniture cushions in a lockable, weather-resistant storage box.

FIVE-MINUTE MAGIC

For easy access to your top gardening tools, place them in a small caddy you can carry from your garage to the garden.

28-Day Challenge

Use this day-by-day guide to tackle each zone and tidy up the house.

Day 1-3: Entryway

Day One Clear your entryway closet of any shoes and coats you do not wear regularly.

Day Two Place umbrellas and cold-weather accessories in labeled bins and stow them at the top of your coat closet.

Day Three Create a drop zone for packages, reminder notes and outgoing mail.

Day 4-6: Living Room

Day Four Clear old titles from your bookshelf and donate them to your local library.

Day Five Assign a place for electronics, be it a caddy for remotes or a movable tray for your game controller.

Day Six Fold throw blankets into stylish baskets.

Day 7-13: Kitchen and Food Storage

Day 7 Stack matching sets of plates, bowls and glasses together.

Day 8 Clear out your under-sink cabinet and fill the area with cleaning essentials like soaps, detergent soaps and multi-purpose sprays.

Day 9 Get utensils in order with a magnetic knife rack, a cooking utensil crock for the counter or drawer dividers for your eating utensils.

Day 10 Toss out old takeout menus, pens that no longer work and old receipts from your junk drawer.

Day 11 Alphabetize your spice collection for easy reference.

Day 12 Toss pantry food that's expired and place similar items together.

Day 13 Clean out your fridge and freezer and discard any expired groceries.

Day 14-18: Bathroom and Laundry Room

Day 14 Place extra cleaning supplies and cosmetics in a clear turntable or plastic bins under your sink.

Day 15 Add an adjustable shower caddy for your shampoos, conditioners and body washes.

Day 16 Roll washcloths into a drawer in your bathroom vanity and fold larger towels in your linen closet.

Day 17 Check the expiration dates of your cosmetics and remove any old items from your collection.

Day 18 Fold bedding sets into a pillowcase for easy access.

Day 19-23: Bedrooms and Closets

Day 19 Sift through clothes and accessories and donate items that no longer fit or are past their prime.

Day 20 Place out-of-season clothes in vacuum-sealed bags and slip them under your bed.

Day 21 Hang up blouses, suits and dresses sorted by style, season or color.

Day 22 Fold and place casual pieces like T-shirts, socks and underwear in closet's drawers or shelves.

Day 23 From untangling necklaces to stuffing shoehorns in fancier shoes, get your accessories in check.

Day 24-28: Spare Space

Day 24 Place toys and craft supplies into labeled baskets.

Day 25 Detangle Christmas lights and folding inflatable yard decorations.

Day 26 If you have an at-home workspace, take an audit of important papers, cables, and office supplies.

Day 27 Create an ongoing file of digital passwords.

Day 28 Install a slat storage system in your garage and hang go-to tools.

Index

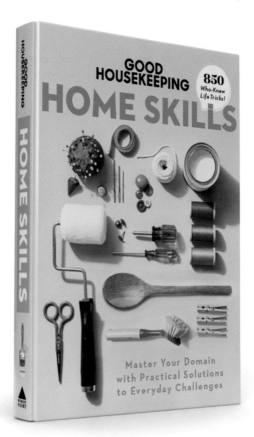

HEARST HOME

Book design by William van Roden

Written by Kelsey Mulvey

Library of Congress Cataloging-in-Publication Data available on request

10 9 8 7 6 5 4 3 2 1

Published by Hearst Home, an imprint of Hearst Books/ Hearst Communications, Inc.

300 W 57th Street

New York, NY 10019

Good Housekeeping, Hearst Home, the Hearst Home logo, and Hearst Books are registered trademarks of Hearst Communications, Inc.

For information about custom editions, special sales, premium and corporate purchases: hearst.com/magazines/ hearst-books

Printed in China

ISBN 978-1-958395-75-2

Cover: Mike Garten (Front), Thomas Kuoh (Back)

365MM/Stocksy/Adobe Stock: 72, 87

AdobeStock: 11, 30, 64, 95, 103–104, 107–108, 111, 126, 135, 155

Aimee Mazzenga: 41, 123

Alison Gootee: 63, 83

Alec Hemer: 57

Alyssa Rosenheck Photography: 149

Andrew McCaul: 96, 130

Annie Schlechter: 47, 101

Cameron Reynolds: 115

Carina Skrobecki: 37

Christopher Dibble: 125

Colin Faulkner: 6, 38, 160

Danielle Daly: 25, 52

Ema Peter: 13

Erika LaPresto: 34

George Barberis: 136

Getty Images: TOC; 33, 55, 58, 68, 71, 78, 81, 88, 112, 129, 139, 140, 143–144, 151–152

Hulya Kolabas: 61

Jacob Snavely: 116, 121

Jeff Herr: 9

Keyanna Bowen: 51

Laura Metzler: 132

Madeline Harper: 14

Max Kim-Bee: 27

Mike Garten: 18, 21, 75, 84, 99, 147

Rachel Whiting: 44

Scott Rickels: 48

Stacy Zarin Goldberg: 17

Thomas Kuoh: 90, 93, 119

Trinette Reed/Stocksy/Adobe Stock: 29, 76

Troy Thies: 42